whispering shrieks

Carson Yenchar

BookLeaf Publishing

Presentation by *BookLeaf Publishing*

Web: www.bookleafpub.com

E-mail: info@bookleafpub.com

ISBN : 9789357699747

First edition 2022

DEDICATION

Dedicated to Harrison, Evan, and Ella; three of the most amazing and talented people I've ever known, never give up your ambitions and keep being yourselves, even when other people tell you not to.
Love you guys.

ACKNOWLEDGEMENT

I would love to acknowledge my family and friends for always supporting me in everything I do, and for always reminding me to keep moving forward and to do the things I love.

A special, special thanks to my high school theatre group for opening my eyes to new possibilities and building up my self-confidence. I couldn't have done it without you.

Another big thanks to my coworkers, who have made me laugh, and getting me through some tough times. Your words of encouragement and love are very much appreciated.

Lastly, thank you to all the dreamers and artists out there, who have given me the inspiration to keep pursuing what I love, and being the light in the darkness. You are all true creators, and I thank you for it.

PREFACE

I have always found that I am able to express myself better through written words. As a shy and often afraid individual, I find courage to let my true feelings through writing from within, and letting the words speak for me. And even in doing so, I have found my voice more and more as I continue to figure out who I am. I only hope that these poems inspire and help people understand themselves in their own ways, as I have found through my own writing. My motto continues to be, "Do things that scare you," for life isn't meant to be led carefully, but rather through taking risks.

flutter, baby

flutter, baby
amongst the wispy winds
flutter, baby
within the pockets of cotton clouds
flutter, baby
like so many before you
color the skies with your wings
fight against the currents of a hurricane
flutter, baby
flutter, baby
cry if you must, but never falter
in your path to freedom
for your strength carries the fallen fools
who dare to live despite it all
flutter high, baby, flutter high

mountain ripples

rocky giants block the sky
their snow-capped tops reflecting off the sun
nothing can escape their view
not even the lone traveler trekking
shadows shift
an eagle cries a great distance
echoing off the grainy walls
and the shadows disperse to light
rippling compressed terrain
providing shelter to the weary traveler
and creature alike
never wavering in its stead
natural beauties but how long can they last
before the inner wealth is cracked
extracted for selfish needs
leaving a hollow shell behind

lynx in the desert

the lynx stalks across the golden land
sniffing the hot air through wet nostrils
mysterious and aloof
the lynx carries its head high
footprints that vanish before they form
the lynx keeps to itself
predator before all else
living to hunt and kill
the lynx spots a rabbit upon the sand
expressions meet in a tug of war
a low growl erupts
while wide eyes dart to and fro
the lynx feels comfort in shared gazes
relaxing muscles, loosening sinews
the lynx trots away whilst the rabbit twitches
watching it slink away into the grains

over the grain fields

over the grain fields
lies more grain
to most people satisfying
but not I
the wind leaves a heavy smell
overwhelming yet familiar
I, for one, have become too familiar
with the likeness of wheat stalks
over the grain fields
perhaps there is a patch of green
open and unfamiliar
but welcoming all the same
grain never lasts
it is harvested for uses like bread and baking
but that is okay
because nothing stays the same anyways

thunderstorms near a lighthouse

wind whips across the ocean waves
surrounding the miniature island
where a isolated lighthouse stands
tipping precariously towards the chaos
a light still shines, despite the desolation
as if fighting to remain conscious
through a growing darkness
overtaking the small vial of bright
nothing lives on the island
besides the spinning light on top
of that brave lighthouse
that shines despite the dangers
cutting a path through the clouds
towards a brand new world

vines falling down

brushing aside the flowing green tendrils
leads to many more
grouped together as if to protect
from the hands grabbing and pulling
sharp objects cut through the strands
causing unearthly moans to escape
only loud enough for neighboring vines
fearing for their lives
take and take, the masses never enough
it's always more, more, more
but the vines cling on
hoping for a long, plentiful peace

fall awakens

green becomes fire
still becomes breeze
the smell of leaves grows
and pumpkins glow a vibrant orange
nothing lasts forever
change often passes by without notice
what is blind to the naked eye
becomes all the more beautiful
scarves unravel at the graying sky
looming ahead or behind, no one knows
but one thing's for certain:
fall awakens, and change happens without
permission

a poet's wisdom

do not dwell on such trivial things
for they will consume you
like ants on a crumb
scavenging for survival
babes are beings with hidden knowledge
we adults lose as we grow
the world seemed so much simpler then
now more of reality shows
but let's open our arms to possibility
although we may falter and tumble
open your mind to new ideas
and let love fill rather than indifference

angry hornets

the hornets buzz in a furious frenzy
feeling nothing but anger
and anger drives the hornet to madness
to judgement upon the unfortunate passerby
why must you screech, hornet?
why must you contradict differences?
isn't the very definition of different
to not be like everyone else?
angry hornets blaze hot rod red
seething, writhing, panting
blinded by the fire within their souls
they feel for nothing nor no one

numbing chill

my fingertips shaded blue
the shine of a freshly washed blueberry
growing darker and darker
as the feeling lessens
numb feels fuzzy, disconnected
your eyes find nothing, and your skin senses
nothing
brain powers down
and noise is foreign to cottony ears
you shiver once, the only reaction
to the overpowering numbness
and once again goes still
who knows when it will pass?

flower showers

upon a certain sunny day
a flower floats to your feet
peeking its head up towards you
asking for guidance
you gaze upon its feathery petals
and gaze harder at the many more flowers
falling from the atmosphere
to the unforgiving ground
the flowers appear to be happy
upon touching solid ground at last
but their stems shrivel despite their joy
and petals snap off, one by one

grow taller

sitting upon a chair
knees drawn to chest in agony
muscles stretching and bones creaking
the pains of growing
my legs grow two feet, I swear
my arms stretch like noodles over my head
I tower high above my desktop
the chair beneath me straining
I stand, my head banging the ceiling
a yelp of pain, then one of shock
at how fast growing begins
and ends

roses and thorns

with beauty comes pain
nothing beautiful ever comes easily
blood will be shed
and loss will be your escort
roses appear beautiful
but can stab upon skin contact
a drop of red dropping into the soil
becoming one with the disguised belle
beauty comes at a great cost
but it can bring peace if found within
rather than the outside
where societal norms dwell

dawn awakenings

a baby is born
a soul is reborn
a tree sprouts leaves on tiny branches
a baby bird cracks through its shell
many mysterious things happen at dawn
things we don't even know about
or maybe aren't supposed to know about
allowing the mystery to remain
dawn swallows the new day
casting spells for new miracles
or new lessons to learn
it awakens the possibilities not yet explored

collecting rocks by the sea

oh, there is a perfectly round specimen
speckled with grays and whites
looking like a bird's egg rather than a rock
but beautiful all the same
another rock hides a hidden gem
quartz, perhaps?
shiny beneath the sandy, dull surface
glowing like a beacon in the sky
rock collecting is a simple hobby
yet tells a story of family and bonding
surfaces representing repressed emotions and thoughts
but rocks remain steadfast, sturdy
in their wake

dizzy love

swimming in nausea-induced rapture
finding one another's eyes across a field
chest heaving with severe trepidation
but alas, a small bloom of hope grows
love never seems to stand still
therefore a great chase pursues
for the right kind of definition
that the word represents
perhaps, love isn't meant to be one entity
but a whole swarm of them
twisting together into a great knot
hoping to be unraveled by lovers young and old

sticks and stones

broken bones
caused by sticks and stones
rather cause one such pain
but so can words in a way
words may not break physically
but mentally, they may
cause such a break that can't be fixed
and would much rather stay
words can be both friend and foe
it is your choice alone
on whether words will build you up
or break you down

misty fog

the air appears hazy and mystical
the time of illusion
fog mists over the land
causing uncertainty and fear
fog is always seen as dangerous
but when cast in faint sunlight
it seems to be alive
in a way that causes hope
it finds two people meeting
for the first time
after years of being together
in vile circumstances

crumpled pages

writings are scarce
when no inspiration appears
instead littered papers scatter
nonsense words spread
too many ideas
all half finished
rough drafts of rough drafts
cycling through and through
i suppose writers are like that
always thinking a mile a minute
coming up with ideas
but never able to finish them

in a dress shop

fabrics swirl upon mannequins
needles bedded in pincushions
soft cotton and satin alike
colors blend to create patterns
mermaid cut and flowing trains
ball gowns expand to unimaginable sizes
taking up the gold cut room
full of mirrors and sparkle
a young boy feels the satin with his cheek
smiling at the softness
that would grace his skin
and bring out his shine at last

marks upon a wall

i have not yet
placed my marks upon the world
for i am waiting
for a moment of peace
although peace never lasts long
there will always be problems
and disagreements in the world
no matter how high the sun sits
so we should be there for others
and take care of those who need us
kindness is rare in this world
so we must build it up ourselves
our marks need not be for our own sake
but for those who have helped and built us up

www.ingramcontent.com/pod-product-compliance
Lightning Source LLC
Chambersburg PA
CBHW062205160726
48282CB00027B/1013
* 9 7 8 9 3 5 7 6 9 9 7 4 7 *